Contents

Chapter 1

Defining Woke Culture

The term "woke" has become a ubiquitous buzzword in today's society, but its meaning is often misinterpreted and misconstrued. To understand the concept of woke culture, it's important to start with a clear definition.

The term "woke" originally emerged from the Black American community as a call to action and awareness, referring to a state of being mentally and emotionally awake to the injustices and inequalities faced by marginalized groups, particularly people of color. However, in recent years, the term has expanded to encompass a wider cultural phenomenon that touches upon various aspects of society, including politics, social media, activism, and even corporate branding.

At its core, woke culture is about being socially and politically conscious and aware, and using that awareness to challenge oppressive systems and advocate for marginalized communities. It's about being vigilant and proactive in the pursuit of justice, equity, and fairness. This often involves taking a critical approach to issues such as race, gender, sexuality, and class, and engaging in activism and activism-adjacent behaviors such as speaking out against injustice, boycotting companies and products that perpetuate harm, and supporting movements and organizations that align with one's values.

However, the rise of woke culture has also led to criticism and backlash from those who view it as overly politically correct, or as a form of censorship that stifles free speech and honest debate. Critics argue that woke culture has created an environment where people are afraid to express their opinions or engage in discourse for fear of being labelled as bigoted or insensitive.

It's important to note that woke culture is not a monolithic entity, and its meaning and scope can vary widely depending on one's perspective and experiences. Some might see it as a necessary response to systemic oppression, while others view it as a form of cultural imperialism that prioritizes certain voices and experiences over others.

Ultimately, the definition of woke culture is a matter of perspective, and its impact on society is a topic of ongoing debate and discussion. But by understanding the roots and motivations behind woke culture, we can engage in a nuanced and informed conversation about its meaning and implications.

Woke culture is a movement that seeks to challenge and dismantle systems of oppression and discrimination, and promote equality and social justice. It's rooted in a recognition that many of the problems faced by marginalized communities are not just individual issues, but are systemic and institutional, and require systemic and institutional solutions.

One of the key features of woke culture is a focus on intersectionality, the idea that various forms of oppression and privilege, such as race, gender, sexuality, and class, are interconnected and cannot be understood in isolation from one another. Intersectionality is a central tenet of woke culture because it recognizes that different people experience oppression and privilege in different ways, and that a one-size-fits-all approach to social justice is insufficient.

Another key aspect of woke culture is its use of language and terminology. Woke culture often involves the adoption of a specific vocabulary and way of speaking that is intended to be more inclusive and sensitive to marginalized communities. This includes avoiding language that is insensitive, offensive, or perpetuates harmful stereotypes, and using terms and phrases that are more empowering and empowering-adjacent, such as "people of color" instead of "minorities."

Woke culture is also closely tied to the rise of social media, which has given people a platform to amplify their voices and share their experiences and perspectives with a wider audience. Social media has allowed the movement to gain traction and reach a global audience, and has played a role in popularizing the term "woke." However, social media has also been criticized for enabling the spread of misinformation and echo chambers, and for creating a culture of performative activism where people post about social justice issues without actually taking concrete actions to support them.

Despite its criticisms, woke culture has had a significant impact on society and has played a role in shaping public discourse and the way we think about issues of justice and equality. Woke culture has given voice to marginalized communities and has helped to raise awareness about the challenges they face. It has also spurred a new generation of activists who are committed to creating a more equitable and just world.

In conclusion, woke culture is a complex and multifaceted phenomenon that touches upon many different aspects of society. Whether one views it as a necessary response to oppression, or as a form of cultural imperialism, its impact on our world is undeniable. By continuing to engage in informed and nuanced discussions about woke culture, we can gain a better understanding of its meaning, implications, and the role it can play in shaping a more equitable and just society.

Chapter 2

The History and Origins of Wokeness

The concept of "wokeness" has its roots in the Black American community and the Civil Rights Movement of the mid-20th century. During this time, activists, scholars, and thinkers were beginning to recognize and challenge the systemic and institutionalized forms of racism and oppression faced by Black Americans.

One of the key figures in the development of wokeness as a cultural movement was Black feminist writer and activist Angela Davis, who wrote about the interconnectedness of various forms of oppression and privilege, and the need for a critical, intersectional approach to social justice. Davis's work helped to lay the foundation for the modern-day understanding of wokeness as a cultural and political phenomenon.

The term "woke" itself has its origins in the African American Vernacular English (AAVE) and originally referred to being "awake" to the injustices and inequalities faced by Black people. This term was popularized in the 1990s and early 2000s by the hip-hop community, where it was used to refer to being socially and politically aware and conscious.

In recent years, the term "woke" has expanded beyond its original usage in the Black American community and has become a widely recognized term across various cultures and communities. With the rise of social media and the increasing visibility of marginalized communities and their experiences, woke culture has gained mainstream recognition and popularity.

However, the mainstreaming of woke culture has also led to criticism and controversy. Some argue that the term has been co-opted by non-Black people, who use it as a way to signal their own progressive values and political correctness, without actually taking concrete actions to support marginalized communities. This has led to a growing sense of scepticism and cynicism towards the term and the concept of wokeness, with some viewing it as a form of performative activism or "virtue signalling."

Despite these criticisms, wokeness remains a powerful and influential cultural and political movement. By continuing to raise awareness about the systemic and institutionalized forms of oppression faced by marginalized communities, and by advocating for social justice and equity, the woke culture movement continues to play a crucial role in shaping the conversation around justice and equality in our society.

The Black Lives Matter (BLM) movement, which emerged in response to the repeated instances of police brutality and violence against Black people, has also played a significant role in the development of the modern-day woke culture. The BLM movement has brought attention to the ongoing struggle for racial justice and equality, and has inspired a new generation of activists and allies to take up the cause.

The term "wokeness" has also been used in relation to other social justice movements, such as the LGBTQ+ rights movement and the feminist movement. These movements have helped to broaden the definition of wokeness to include a greater understanding of the intersections of various forms of oppression and privilege.

The concept of intersectionality, first introduced by Black feminist scholar Kimberlé Crenshaw, is a key aspect of woke culture. Intersectionality refers to the ways in which different forms of oppression and privilege intersect and compound to create unique experiences of oppression for individuals and communities. Wokeness emphasizes the importance of understanding and recognizing the intersections of race, gender, sexuality, class, ability, and other forms of identity in the pursuit of social justice.

The rise of digital media and social media has played a significant role in the popularization of woke culture. Social media platforms have given marginalized communities a platform to share their experiences, amplify their voices, and organize for change. This has allowed the ideas and values of woke culture to reach a wider audience and gain greater visibility and recognition.

Despite the positive aspects of woke culture, it is important to recognize that the pursuit of social justice is a complex and ongoing process, and that wokeness is not a monolithic or static concept. Wokeness is constantly evolving and changing as new forms of oppression and privilege emerge, and as new generations of activists and allies bring their own perspectives and experiences to the movement.

Overall, the history and origins of wokeness are rich and complex, reflecting the ongoing struggle for justice and equality in our society. By examining the roots of this cultural and political movement, we can gain a deeper understanding of the challenges and opportunities facing marginalized communities, and work towards a more equitable and just future for all.

Chapter 3

Wokeness in the Media and Entertainment Industry

The media and entertainment industry has a significant impact on shaping public perceptions and attitudes, and has played an important role in the popularization and mainstreaming of the woke culture movement. From television shows and movies, to music and social media, the media and entertainment industry has increasingly embraced themes of social justice and diversity, reflecting the growing influence of wokeness in our culture.

One of the key ways that the media and entertainment industry has reflected the values of wokeness is through the increasing representation of marginalized communities and experiences in the media. This has included more diverse representation in television shows and movies, with characters of different races, genders, sexualities, and abilities, as well as stories that highlight the experiences and struggles of these communities. This greater representation has helped to bring visibility and recognition to the experiences of marginalized communities, and has helped to challenge and break down harmful stereotypes and prejudices.

The media and entertainment industry has also played a role in shaping public discourse and opinions around social justice issues, by raising awareness and fostering critical thinking around these topics. This has included the use of documentaries, films, and television shows to highlight important social justice issues, such as police brutality, the refugee crisis, and climate change. By bringing these issues to the forefront of public consciousness, the media and entertainment industry has helped to promote greater understanding and compassion for marginalized communities and the challenges they face.

In addition to reflecting the values of wokeness, the media and entertainment industry has also become a target of criticism from some who argue that its attempts to be politically correct and socially conscious are often superficial and performative, rather than genuine and meaningful. This criticism has been particularly pronounced in the music and entertainment industry, where some argue that the increasing emphasis on "wokeness" is a marketing ploy, designed to appeal to younger and more socially conscious audiences.

Despite these criticisms, the impact of wokeness in the media and entertainment industry remains significant, and its influence is only likely to grow in the years to come. By continuing to promote greater representation, understanding, and critical thinking around social justice issues, the media and entertainment industry has the potential to play a powerful role in shaping public perceptions and attitudes, and promoting greater social justice and equity in our society.

The media and entertainment industry has played a significant role in the popularization and mainstreaming of the woke culture movement. From greater representation of marginalized communities, to raising awareness and fostering critical thinking around social justice issues, the media and entertainment industry has helped to shape public discourse and promote greater understanding and compassion for marginalized communities. Despite its criticisms and controversies, the impact of wokeness in the media and entertainment industry remains significant, and its influence will continue to be felt for years to come.

The media and entertainment industry's influence on shaping public perception and attitudes cannot be overstated. It has become a powerful tool for both promoting and critiquing the values of wokeness.

One example of the media industry promoting wokeness can be seen in the rise of diversity and representation initiatives in Hollywood. Studios and production companies have made a concerted effort to increase the representation of marginalized communities in front of and behind the camera. This has included casting more actors of color, women, and members of the LGBTQ+ community in lead roles, as well as hiring more directors, producers, and writers from these communities. This increased representation has not only helped to promote greater understanding and compassion for marginalized communities, but has also challenged harmful stereotypes and prejudices that have long perpetuated in the media.

Another example of the media industry promoting wokeness can be seen in the use of documentaries and films to raise awareness about social justice issues. These works often use powerful storytelling to highlight the experiences of marginalized communities and to shed light on issues such as police brutality, systemic racism, and the refugee crisis. By bringing these important issues to the forefront of public consciousness, these works can help to foster critical thinking and greater empathy for those affected by these issues.

However, the media and entertainment industry has also faced criticism for its attempts to be politically correct and socially conscious. Some have argued that these efforts are often superficial and performative, rather than genuine and meaningful. For instance, some have criticized the music industry for using the language of social justice and diversity as a marketing tool, in order to appeal to younger and more socially conscious audiences.

Despite these criticisms, the influence of wokeness in the media and entertainment industry remains significant. As society continues to grapple with complex social justice issues, the media and entertainment industry will continue to play a critical role in shaping public perceptions and attitudes, and promoting greater understanding and empathy for marginalized communities.

In conclusion, the media and entertainment industry has played a crucial role in both promoting and critiquing the values of wokeness. Its efforts to increase representation, raise awareness about social justice issues, and foster critical thinking, have helped to shape public discourse and promote greater equity and understanding in our society. However, it has also faced criticism for being performative in its attempts to be politically correct and socially conscious. Despite these criticisms, the impact of wokeness in the media and entertainment industry remains significant, and its influence will continue to be felt for years to come.

Chapter 4

Wokeness in the Workplace

Wokeness has increasingly become a relevant topic in the workplace, as companies strive to create inclusive and diverse environments. The push for wokeness in the workplace has been driven by a growing awareness of the importance of diversity and inclusivity in the business world, as well as the recognition of the tangible benefits that come from promoting these values.

One of the key ways that wokeness has impacted the workplace is through the implementation of diversity and inclusion initiatives. These initiatives often focus on increasing representation and improving the experiences of underrepresented groups, such as people of color, women, and members of the LGBTQ+ community. Companies have sought to achieve these goals through a range of measures, such as creating employee resource groups, promoting diversity in hiring, and implementing unconscious bias training.

Another way that wokeness has impacted the workplace is through the promotion of social justice causes. Many companies have made public statements about their commitment to addressing issues such as racial injustice, climate change, and LGBTQ+ rights. Some companies have also taken concrete steps to support these causes, such as partnering with advocacy organizations, making financial contributions, and advocating for policies that promote social justice.

However, despite the positive impact that wokeness has had in the workplace, it has also faced criticism. Some have argued that the focus on wokeness has led to a culture of political correctness, in which employees are afraid to express their opinions for fear of being labelled as insensitive or bigoted. Others have claimed that the promotion of wokeness in the workplace can be divisive, and that it can lead to resentment among employees who do not share these values.

Wokeness has had a significant impact on the workplace, as companies strive to create inclusive and diverse environments. Through diversity and inclusion initiatives, and the promotion of social justice causes, companies have sought to improve the experiences of underrepresented groups and create more equitable workplaces. However, these efforts have also faced criticism, and it remains to be seen how the push for wokeness in the workplace will continue to evolve in the future. Nevertheless, the trend towards wokeness in the workplace is likely to persist, as companies seek to respond to the changing values and expectations of their employees and society at large.

While some see the promotion of wokeness in the workplace as a positive step towards creating more inclusive and diverse environments, others view it with scepticism. Critics argue that the focus on wokeness can be stifling to free speech and open discourse, and that it can create a culture of political correctness in which employees are afraid to express their opinions for fear of being labelled as insensitive or bigoted.

Another concern is that the promotion of wokeness in the workplace can be divisive, creating resentment among employees who do not share these values. For example, employees who come from conservative backgrounds or hold traditional values may feel that their views are not represented or valued in a workplace that is focused on promoting progressive causes. This can create tension and even conflicts among co-workers, and can negatively impact the overall workplace culture.

However, proponents of wokeness in the workplace argue that these concerns are overstated and that the benefits of promoting these values far outweigh the risks. They argue that creating a workplace culture that is inclusive and supportive of diversity can improve employee satisfaction and engagement, and can also lead to increased innovation and creativity. This is because a diverse workplace brings together employees with different perspectives and experiences, which can lead to new and creative solutions to business problems.

In conclusion, the promotion of wokeness in the workplace is a complex and nuanced issue, with valid arguments on both sides. While some see it as a positive step towards creating more inclusive and diverse environments, others worry that it can stifle free speech and create resentment among employees who do not share these values. Ultimately, the best approach may be to find a balance between promoting wokeness in the workplace and allowing employees to freely express their opinions and ideas.

Chapter 5

Wokeness and Activism

Wokeness and activism have become closely intertwined in recent years, as people seek to use their voices and actions to bring about positive change in the world. At its core, wokeness is about being aware of and actively combating social injustices, and activism is the means by which this is achieved.

One of the key ways that wokeness and activism intersect is through social media. Social media platforms have provided a powerful tool for people to raise awareness about important issues and to mobilize others to take action. For example, hashtags such as #BlackLivesMatter and #MeToo have become synonymous with activism, and have helped to spark widespread social and political movements.

Another way that wokeness and activism intersect is through protests and demonstrations. Protests have long been a powerful form of activism, allowing people to gather together and make their voices heard. In recent years, there have been many high-profile protests around the world, such as the Women's March, the March for Our Lives, and the Climate Strike, that have brought together large numbers of people to call for change.

However, not everyone is a fan of wokeness and activism. Critics argue that the push for wokeness can be divisive, and that it can lead to a culture of political correctness in which people are afraid to express their opinions for fear of being labelled as insensitive or bigoted. Some also argue that activism can be disruptive, and that it can interfere with the functioning of society.

Despite these criticisms, wokeness and activism show no signs of slowing down. As social and political issues continue to evolve, it is likely that people will continue to use their voices and actions to bring about positive change in the world. In this sense, wokeness and activism can be seen as a powerful force for good, helping to create a more equitable and just society for all.

Wokeness and activism are closely related, as people seek to use their voices and actions to bring about positive change in the world. Whether through social media, protests and demonstrations, or other means, activism is a powerful tool for promoting social justice and combating social injustices. While it is not without its critics, the trend towards wokeness and activism is likely to persist, as people seek to make their mark on the world and create a better future for all.

Wokeness and activism have become a defining feature of our time, as people seek to bring about change and create a more just and equitable society. The intersection of these two concepts is particularly important in understanding the current political and cultural landscape, as more and more people become politically and socially conscious.

One of the key ways that wokeness and activism intersect is through education. For many, becoming woke is a process of self-discovery, in which they learn about the systemic inequalities and injustices that exist in society. This education often leads to a desire to take action, and to become an activist in one form or another. Whether through joining a political campaign, volunteering for a social justice organization.

Wokeness and activism have also become a key part of corporate and business culture. As consumers become increasingly concerned about the social and environmental impact of the products they buy, companies are responding by adopting more socially responsible policies and practices. For example, many companies have begun to incorporate sustainability into their business models, and to source materials from environmentally responsible suppliers.

In the workplace, wokeness and activism can also take the form of diversity, equity, and inclusion initiatives. Companies are increasingly recognizing the importance of creating inclusive and welcoming work environments, where employees from all backgrounds feel valued and respected. This often involves providing training and education on issues of diversity, equity, and inclusion, as well as promoting diversity and inclusion in the hiring process and throughout the company culture.

However, the intersection of wokeness and activism is not without its challenges. There are those who argue that businesses should not become involved in political and social issues, and that activism in the workplace can be disruptive and divisive. Others argue that corporate activism is often little more than lip service, and that companies are more concerned with protecting their reputation than with creating real change.

Despite these challenges, the trend towards wokeness and activism in the workplace is likely to continue, as consumers and employees increasingly demand that companies take a more active role in promoting social and environmental responsibility. As a result, businesses and corporations will play an increasingly important role in shaping the future of activism and in creating a more just and equitable society.

In conclusion, the intersection of wokeness and activism has become a key part of our culture, influencing everything from the media and entertainment industry to the workplace. Whether through education, activism, or corporate social responsibility, wokeness and activism will continue to shape our world, as people seek to create a better future for all.

Chapter 6

The Political Aspects of Wokeness

The political aspects of wokeness have become increasingly prominent in recent years, as individuals and communities become more politically conscious and engaged. This has led to the rise of a new generation of political activists and advocates, who are using their voices to bring about change and create a more just and equitable society.

One of the key ways that wokeness intersects with politics is through activism. Woke individuals often become politically active, either through participating in political campaigns or movements, or through speaking out on political issues through social media and other forms of communication. This activism can take many forms, from peaceful protest and demonstration, to more direct forms of political action such as lobbying and advocacy.

In addition to activism, wokeness has also influenced the political landscape through the rise of identity politics. Wokeness often emphasizes the importance of understanding and addressing the experiences of marginalized communities, including people of color, the LGBTQ+ community, and those with disabilities. This has led to the growth of political movements centred around these experiences, as well as to a growing awareness of the need to address the systemic inequalities and injustices that affect these communities.

However, the political aspects of wokeness have also been met with opposition. Critics argue that wokeness is overly politically correct and that it stifles free speech and open debate. Some also argue that wokeness has become too focused on individual experiences and identities, rather than on broader political and social issues.

Despite these criticisms, the trend towards wokeness and political engagement is likely to continue, as more and more people become politically conscious and seek to bring about change. As a result, wokeness and activism will continue to play a significant role in shaping the political landscape, as individuals and communities seek to create a more just and equitable society.

The relationship between wokeness and politics is complex and multifaceted, encompassing everything from individual activism to the rise of new political movements. Wokeness has had a profound impact on the political landscape, driving changes in public opinion, shaping political discourse, and influencing policy decisions.

One of the most significant ways that wokeness has impacted politics is through the rise of social justice activism. Woke individuals are often politically engaged and actively working to address the inequalities and injustices that exist in society. This activism can take many forms, from peaceful demonstrations and marches, to more direct forms of political action such as lobbying, advocacy, and petitioning. Through their activism, woke individuals are working to bring about change and create a more just and equitable world.

In addition to activism, wokeness has also influenced the political landscape through the rise of identity politics. Wokeness often emphasizes the importance of understanding and addressing the experiences of marginalized communities, including people of color, the LGBTQ+ community, and those with disabilities. This has led to the growth of political movements centred around these experiences, as well as to a growing awareness of the need to address the systemic inequalities and injustices that affect these communities.

However, the political aspects of wokeness have also been met with opposition. Critics argue that wokeness is overly politically correct and that it stifles free speech and open debate. Some also argue that wokeness has become too focused on individual experiences and identities, rather than on broader political and social issues.

Despite these criticisms, the trend towards wokeness and political engagement is likely to continue, as more and more people become politically conscious and seek to bring about change. This will likely result in the growth of social justice activism and the continued rise of identity politics.

In addition to activism and identity politics, wokeness has also impacted the political landscape through its influence on the media and popular culture. The media and entertainment industry has become increasingly woke, with many companies and content creators actively promoting and amplifying the voices of marginalized communities. This has helped to increase awareness and understanding of these experiences, and has played a significant role in shaping public opinion and driving political change.

In conclusion, the political aspects of wokeness are a complex and multifaceted phenomenon, impacting everything from activism and political engagement, to the rise of identity politics and the media and entertainment industry. Whether through activism, advocacy, or the promotion of marginalized voices, wokeness will continue to play an important role in shaping the political landscape and in creating a better future for all.

Chapter 7

The Controversies Surrounding Wokeness

Wokeness has been the subject of much debate and controversy in recent years, with opinions ranging from enthusiastic support to staunch opposition. While many view wokeness as a positive movement towards a more equitable and just society, others argue that it has gone too far and is having negative consequences for society and individuals alike.

One of the main controversies surrounding wokeness is the issue of political correctness. Critics argue that the focus on being politically correct has stifled free speech and open debate, with individuals afraid to express their opinions for fear of being labelled as insensitive or intolerant. Some also argue that the emphasis on political correctness has created a culture of outrage and cancel culture, where individuals are publicly shamed and even fired from their jobs for making insensitive remarks or taking actions that are deemed unacceptable by the woke community.

Another controversy surrounding wokeness is its impact on the workplace. While many companies have embraced wokeness and made it a priority, some employees have reported feeling pressured to conform to certain political views and to avoid certain topics of conversation. This has led to concerns about the negative impact on workplace diversity and free speech, as well as the potential for discrimination against individuals who hold different political views.

The relationship between wokeness and activism has also been a source of controversy. While many view wokeness as a positive force for change and activism, others argue that it has become too focused on individual experiences and identities, rather than on broader social and political issues. This has led to criticism that wokeness has become more about being seen as politically correct, rather than actually effecting meaningful change.

Wokeness has also been criticized for its impact on race relations. Some argue that the focus on individual experiences and identities has led to increased division and a "victim mentality," rather than promoting unity and understanding. Others argue that the emphasis on racial identities has led to reverse discrimination and has reinforced existing stereotypes and prejudices.

In addition to the controversies already discussed, the concept of "virtue signalling" has also been a source of criticism surrounding wokeness. Critics argue that individuals often use wokeness as a way to publicly demonstrate their political correctness and moral superiority, rather than as a genuine commitment to activism and change. This has led to concerns that wokeness has become more about performative activism and self-promotion, rather than meaningful engagement and action.

Another controversy surrounding wokeness is its impact on education. Some argue that the emphasis on political correctness in educational institutions has stifled free speech and intellectual inquiry, with individuals afraid to express controversial or unconventional ideas. Additionally, some argue that the focus on wokeness in education has led to a neglect of important subjects and skills, such as critical thinking and objective analysis.

Wokeness has also been criticized for its impact on mental health and well-being. Some argue that the pressure to conform to certain political views and to avoid certain topics of conversation can lead to stress and anxiety, as well as a sense of disconnection and isolation from others. Additionally, the focus on individual experiences and identities can reinforce negative self-perceptions and lead to feelings of inadequacy and insecurity.

It is important to note that these controversies are not unique to wokeness, but are also present in other social and political movements. Additionally, while some of these criticisms are valid and should be taken into account, it is also important to recognize the positive aspects of wokeness, such as its potential to promote empathy, understanding, and social justice.

In conclusion, the controversies surrounding wokeness are complex and multifaceted, and reflect a broader debate about the role of political correctness, activism, and social justice in society. It is important to continue the discussion and debate surrounding wokeness and to carefully consider its impact on society and individuals, in order to arrive at a better understanding of this complex and evolving phenomenon.

Chapter 8

Wokeness and Education

The relationship between wokeness and education is a complex and often controversial one. On the one hand, wokeness has the potential to promote important values such as empathy, understanding, and social justice in educational institutions. For example, by incorporating a critical examination of issues such as systemic racism and oppression into the curriculum, students can gain a deeper understanding of the complexities of these issues and develop the skills and knowledge necessary to work towards creating a more equitable society.

However, the integration of wokeness into education has also been the source of criticism and controversy. Some argue that the focus on wokeness has led to a neglect of important subjects and skills, such as critical thinking and objective analysis. Additionally, the emphasis on political correctness in educational institutions has been criticized for stifling free speech and intellectual inquiry, with individuals afraid to express controversial or unconventional ideas.

Another issue surrounding wokeness and education is the concept of "cancel culture," or the phenomenon of individuals being ostracized or "cancelled" for expressing views that are considered to be insensitive, offensive, or not politically correct. This has led to concerns that students and educators may be afraid to engage in honest and open discussions about difficult topics, for fear of being labelled as "not woke" or facing social or professional consequences.

In order to address these concerns and ensure that wokeness is integrated into education in a positive and effective manner, it is important to strike a balance between promoting social justice and critical thinking. This can be achieved by encouraging open and honest discussions about difficult topics, while also promoting the development of critical thinking skills and an appreciation for diverse perspectives. Additionally, it is important to recognize the importance of free speech and intellectual inquiry in educational institutions, and to work towards creating a supportive and inclusive learning environment where all individuals feel free to express their opinions and ideas.

One aspect of wokeness in education that deserves further examination is the role of teachers and instructors in promoting a "woke" education. These individuals play a critical role in shaping the way that students understand and engage with the world around them, and their views on wokeness and social justice can have a significant impact on the way that these subjects are taught and understood.

One approach that has been taken in some schools and universities is to incorporate social justice and "woke" education into teacher training programs. This can help to ensure that teachers have a solid understanding of these concepts and are equipped to incorporate them into their teaching practices in a meaningful and effective manner. Additionally, teachers can also be encouraged to engage in ongoing professional development to stay current with the latest research and developments in these areas.

Another important aspect of wokeness in education is the use of technology and digital media in promoting social justice and "wokeness." The widespread availability of digital media has allowed for the rapid dissemination of information and ideas, and has provided new opportunities for individuals to engage with social justice issues. For example, students can use social media to connect with like-minded individuals, to access resources and information about social justice issues, and to engage in activism and advocacy.

In addition to these opportunities, there are also significant challenges associated with the use of technology in promoting wokeness in education. For example, the spread of misinformation and "fake news" can make it difficult for students to differentiate between credible and credible sources of information. Additionally, there are concerns about the potential for online harassment and bullying, as well as the impact that the constant exposure to social media can have on mental health and well-being.

Ultimately, the relationship between wokeness and education is a complex and multifaceted one, and it is important to approach it with care and consideration. By working to ensure that teachers and instructors have a solid understanding of these concepts and are equipped to promote them in the classroom, and by utilizing technology in a responsible and effective manner, we can help to create an educational system that promotes equity, understanding, and social justice.

In conclusion, the intersection of wokeness and education presents both opportunities and challenges. By promoting a "woke" education, teachers and instructors can play a critical role in shaping the way that students understand and engage with the world around them, and in promoting equity, understanding, and social justice. However, it is important to approach this relationship with care and consideration, to ensure that the use of technology and digital media is responsible and effective, and to address the challenges associated with misinformation and online harassment. Ultimately, the goal of a "wokeness" education should be to empower students to critically engage with the world around them, and to equip them with the tools and knowledge they need to make a positive impact in their communities and in society at large.

Chapter 9

Wokeness and Mental Health

The relationship between wokeness and mental health is a complex and multifaceted one. On one hand, wokeness can provide individuals with a sense of purpose, community, and a sense of belonging. By engaging in activism and advocacy, individuals can feel empowered to make a positive impact in their communities and in society at large.

However, the constant exposure to social justice issues and the pressure to be "woke" can also have negative impacts on mental health and well-being. For example, individuals who are highly engaged in activism and advocacy may experience feelings of overwhelm and burnout as they attempt to navigate complex and often contentious social justice issues. Additionally, the constant exposure to traumatic or distressing content through social media and other forms of media can have a profound impact on mental health, contributing to symptoms of anxiety, depression, and post-traumatic stress disorder.

One aspect of the relationship between wokeness and mental health that is particularly relevant to consider is the impact of online activism and advocacy. The use of social media and other digital platforms has allowed for the rapid dissemination of information and ideas, and has provided new opportunities for individuals to engage with social justice issues. However, the constant exposure to traumatic or distressing content, as well as the potential for online harassment and bullying, can have a significant impact on mental health and well-being.

It is also important to consider the impact of microaggressions and discrimination on the mental health of individuals who are part of marginalized communities. These individuals may experience repeated instances of microaggressions, discrimination, and other forms of trauma, which can contribute to feelings of anxiety, depression, and other mental health concerns.

In order to promote positive mental health outcomes for individuals who are engaged in wokeness and activism, it is important to prioritize self-care and to engage in regular self-reflection. This can include setting healthy boundaries with technology and social media, seeking out supportive community and social networks, and engaging in self-care activities such as exercise, meditation, and therapy.

Additionally, it is also important to promote a culture of care and support within activism and advocacy communities. This can include providing resources and support for individuals who are experiencing mental health concerns, and promoting a culture of inclusivity and understanding.

Ultimately, the relationship between wokeness and mental health is a complex and nuanced one. By prioritizing self-care and promoting a culture of care and support within activism and advocacy communities, we can help to ensure that individuals who are engaged in these pursuits are able to maintain positive mental health outcomes.

It's important to note that the relationship between wokeness and mental health is not a one-size-fits-all scenario. Different individuals may experience different outcomes depending on their unique experiences, identities, and perspectives.

For example, for individuals who are part of marginalized communities, wokeness may provide a sense of validation, empowerment, and hope. By engaging in activism and advocacy, these individuals can find a sense of community, belonging, and purpose, which can have a positive impact on their mental health and well-being.

However, for individuals who are not part of these communities, the constant exposure to social justice issues and the pressure to be "woke" may lead to feelings of anxiety, guilt, and stress. These individuals may feel overwhelmed by the sheer number and complexity of social justice issues, and may struggle to reconcile their own experiences and beliefs with the messages they are exposed to through the media and social media.

It's also important to consider the impact of wokeness on the mental health of individuals who are on the receiving end of activism and advocacy efforts. For example, individuals who are accused of perpetuating prejudice, discrimination, or microaggressions may experience feelings of anger, frustration, and shame, which can have a significant impact on their mental health and well-being.

In order to promote positive mental health outcomes for individuals who are engaged in wokeness and activism, it is important to prioritize open, honest, and non-judgmental discussions about the relationship between these pursuits and mental health. This can include engaging in regular self-reflection and self-care, seeking out support from trusted friends, family members, or mental health professionals, and promoting a culture of care and understanding within activism and advocacy communities.

It's also important to note that mental health is not a personal issue, but a social issue that is shaped by the cultural, political, and economic contexts in which we live. As such, it's important to address the root causes of mental health issues, including poverty, discrimination, and marginalization, in order to promote positive mental health outcomes for all individuals.

In conclusion, the relationship between wokeness and mental health is a complex and multifaceted one that is shaped by a range of individual, cultural, and contextual factors. By prioritizing self-care, seeking out support, and promoting a culture of care and understanding within activism and advocacy communities, we can help to ensure that individuals who are engaged in these pursuits are able to maintain positive mental health outcomes.

Chapter 10

The Future of Wokeness: Predictions and Possibilities

In the final chapter of our book, we will take a look at the future of wokeness and what it may hold. Wokeness, as a cultural and social phenomenon, has seen significant growth and development over the past few decades. With the ongoing evolution of technology, media, and communication, it is safe to say that wokeness is here to stay and is likely to continue to influence various aspects of our lives in new and exciting ways.

One of the primary areas where we can expect to see the continued influence of wokeness is in activism and social justice movements. As more and more people become aware of and educated about issues such as race, gender, and sexuality, the demand for progress and change will only increase. Wokeness has already played a significant role in bringing about significant social and political change, and this trend is likely to continue in the coming years.

Another area where we can expect to see the growth of wokeness is in the workplace. With the rise of remote work and virtual offices, companies and organizations will need to be increasingly mindful of their employees' well-being and mental health. Wokeness, with its focus on creating a safe and inclusive environment, is likely to play a crucial role in shaping the future of work.

Wokeness may also impact education in the coming years. As more schools and universities strive to create a more diverse and inclusive environment, the principles of wokeness are likely to play a significant role in shaping their curriculums, policies, and practices. The focus on creating a more equitable and just society will continue to drive the development of educational programs and initiatives that promote diversity, equity, and inclusion.

It's also worth considering the role that technology will play in shaping the future of wokeness. The rise of social media has already allowed people to connect and mobilize around causes they care about in new and unprecedented ways. In the coming years, we can expect to see the continued growth of virtual activism and social justice movements, as well as the increased use of technology to raise awareness and bring about change.

Moreover, the increasing trend towards personalized and experiential learning may also shape the future of wokeness in education. Instead of a one-size-fits-all approach, educational institutions may begin to offer more tailored and customized programs that are aligned with the specific needs and interests of students. This shift could lead to a more inclusive and diverse learning environment, as students from different backgrounds and experiences can benefit from programs that are designed to meet their unique needs.

In addition, it's also worth exploring the relationship between wokeness and mental health. As we've discussed earlier, wokeness can sometimes lead to feelings of burnout, anxiety, and stress, especially among those who are actively engaged in activism and social justice movements. As a result, it's crucial that we continue to address and address these concerns and find ways to support and care for individuals who are working towards creating a more just and equitable world.

In conclusion, the future of wokeness is uncertain, but it's clear that the principles of wokeness will continue to play a critical role in shaping various aspects of our lives. As we move forward, it's important that we remain open-minded and continue to critically examine and engage with the complexities of wokeness, while also working to create a more just and equitable world for all. Whether through activism and social justice movements, the workplace, education, or technology, the future of wokeness holds immense potential for growth and progress, and it's up to us to ensure that this potential is realized.